Mohammed And Cosmic

Consciousness

Ali Nomad

Kessinger Publishing's Rare Reprints

Thousands of Scarce and Hard-to-Find Books
on These and other Subjects!

- Americana
- Ancient Mysteries
- Animals
- Anthropology
- Architecture
- Arts
- Astrology
- Bibliographies
- Biographies & Memoirs
- Body, Mind & Spirit
- Business & Investing
- Children & Young Adult
- Collectibles
- Comparative Religions
- Crafts & Hobbies
- Earth Sciences
- Education
- Ephemera
- Fiction
- Folklore
- Geography
- Health & Diet
- History
- Hobbies & Leisure
- Humor
- Illustrated Books
- Language & Culture
- Law
- Life Sciences

- Literature
- Medicine & Pharmacy
- Metaphysical
- Music
- Mystery & Crime
- Mythology
- Natural History
- Outdoor & Nature
- Philosophy
- Poetry
- Political Science
- Science
- Psychiatry & Psychology
- Reference
- Religion & Spiritualism
- Rhetoric
- Sacred Books
- Science Fiction
- Science & Technology
- Self-Help
- Social Sciences
- Symbolism
- Theatre & Drama
- Theology
- Travel & Explorations
- War & Military
- Women
- Yoga
- *Plus Much More!*

We kindly invite you to view our catalog list at:
http://www.kessinger.net

CHAPTER XI

MAHOMMED

Despite the fact that the followers of Mahommed, the prophet, are among the most fanatical and prejudiced of all religious sects, Mahommed himself was unquestionably among·the Illumined Ones of earth, and had attained and retained a high degree of cosmic consciousness.

The wars; the persecutions; the horrors that have been committed in the name of Islam, are perhaps a little more atrocious than any in history although the unspeakable cruelties of the Inquisition would seem to have no parallel.

The religion of Persia, wrongly alluded to as "fire-worship," marks Zoroaster as among the Illuminati, but as the present volume is concerned, in the religious aspect of it, only with those cases of Illumination which we are classifying among the present great religious systems, we cite the case of Mahommed, the Arab, as one clearly establishing the characteristic points of Illumination.

When Mahommed was born, in the early part of the fifth century, the condition of his countrymen was primitive in the extreme.

The most powerful force among them was tribal or clan loyalty, and a corresponding hatred of, and readiness to make war with, opposing clans.

Although at the time of Mahommed's birth, Christianity had made great headway in different parts of the old world, it had made very little impress upon the Arabs. They worshipped their tribal gods, and there are traces of a belief in a supreme God (Allah ta-ala), but they were not as a race inclined to a deeply religious sentiment.

One and all, whether given to superstitions or denying a belief in Allah, they dreaded the dark after-life and although the different tribes made their yearly pilgrimages to Mecca, and faithfully kissed the stone that had fallen from heaven in the days of Adam, the inspiration of their ancient prophets had long since died, and a new prophet was expected and looked for.

The yearly pilgrimage to Mecca, which was at once the center of trade and the goal of the religious enthusiast, was observed by all the tribes of Arabia, but it is a question whether the pilgrimage was not more often made in a holiday spirit than in that of the devotee to the *Kaabeh*, the most sacred temple in all Arabia.

Indeed, it is agreed by all commentators, that the ancient Arab, "In the Time of Ignorance," before the coming of Mahommed, knew little and cared less about those spiritual qualities that look beyond the physical; not questioning, as did Mahommed, what lies beyond this vale of strife, whose only exit is the dark and inscrutable face of death.

Besides the tribal gods, individual households had their special Penates, to whom was due the first and the last salam of the returning or outgoing host. But in spite of all this superstitious apparatus, the Arabs were never a religious people. In the old days, as now, they were reckless, skeptical, materialistic. They had their gods and their divining arrows, but they were ready to demolish both if the responses proved contrary to their wishes. A great majority believed in no future life, nor in a reckoning day of good and evil.

Such, then, was the condition of thought among the various tribes when Mahommed was born.

It was not, however, until he was past forty years of age, that the revelations came to him, and although it was some time later that these were set down, together with his admonitions and counsel to his followers, it is believed that they are for the most part well authenticated, as the Koran was compiled during Mahommed's lifetime, and thus, in the original, doubtless represents an authentic account of Mahommed's experiences.

It is related that Mahommed's father died before his son's birth and his mother six years later. Thus Mahommed was left to the care of his grandfather, the virtual chief of Mecca. The venerable chief lived but two years and Mahommed, who was a great favorite with his grandfather, became the special charge of his uncle, Aboo-Talib, whose devotion never wavered, even during the trying later years, when Mahommed's persecutions caused the uncle untold hardships and trials.

At an early age Mahommed took up the life of a sheep herder, caring for the herds of his kinsmen. This step became necessary because the once princely fortune of his noble ancestors had dwindled to almost the extreme of poverty, but although the occupation of sheep herder was despised by the tribes, it is said that Mahommed himself in later life often alluded to his early calling as the time when "God called him."

At the age of twenty-five he took up the more desirable post of camel driver, and was taken into the employ of a wealthy kinswoman, Khadeejeh, whom he afterwards married, although she was fifteen years his senior—a disparity in age which means far more in the East, where physical charm and beauty are the only requisites for a wife, than it does in the West where men

look more to the mental endowments of a wife
than to the fleeting charm of youth.

It is also to Mahommed's credit that his devotion to his first wife never wavered to the day of
her death and, indeed, as long as he himself lived
he spoke with reverence and deep affection of
Khadeejeh.

. We learn that the next fifteen years were lived
in the usual manner of a man of his station.
Khadeejeh brought him wealth and this gave him
the necessary time and ease in which to medi-
tate, and the never-varying devotion and trust of
his faithful wife brought him repose and the
power to aid his impoverished uncle, and to be
regarded among the tribes as a man of influence.

His simple, unostentatious, and even ascetic
life during these years was noted. He was
known as a man of extremely refined tastes and
sensitive though not querulous nature. A com-
mentator says of him:

"His constitution was extremely delicate. He
was nervously afraid of bodily pain; he would
sob and roar under it. Eminently unpractical in
the common things of life, he was gifted with
mighty powers of imagination, elevation of mind,
delicacy and refinement of feeling. "He is more
modest than a virgin behind her curtain," it has
been said of him.

"He was most indulgent to his inferiors and

would not allow his awkward little page to be scolded, whatever he did. He was most affectionate toward his family. He was very fond of children, and would stop them in the streets and pat their little cheeks. He never struck anyone in his life. The worst expression he ever made use of in conversation was: 'What has come to him—may his forehead be darkened with mud.'

"When asked to curse some one he replied: 'I have not been sent to curse, but to be a mercy to mankind.' He visited the sick, followed any bier he met, accepted the invitation of a slave to dinner, mended his own clothes, milked his goats and waited upon himself.

"He never withdrew his hand out of another's palm, and turned not before the other had turned.

"He was the most faithful protector of those he protected, the sweetest and most agreeable in conversation; those who saw him were suddenly filled with reverence; those who came to him, loved him. They who described him would say: 'I have never seen his like, either before or after.'

"He was, however, very nervous and restless withal, often low-spirited, downcast as to heart and eyes. Yet he would at times suddenly break through these broodings, become gay, talkative, jocular, chiefly among his own."

This picture corresponds with the temperament which is alluded to as the "artistic," or "psychic" temperament, and allowing that in these days there is much posing and pretense, we still must admit that the quality known as "temperament" is a psychological study suggesting a stage of development hitherto unclassified. It is said also, that in his youth Mahommed was subject to attacks of catalepsy, evidencing an organism peculiarly "psychic."

It is evident that Mahommed regarded himself as one having a mission upon earth, even before he had received the revelations which announced him as a prophet chosen of Allah, for he long brooded over the things of the spirit, and although he had not, up to his fortieth year, openly protested against the fetish worship of the Kureysh, yet he was regarded as one who had a different idea of worship from that of the men with whom he came in contact.

Gradually, he became more and more inclined to solitude, and made frequent excursions into the hills, and in his solitary wanderings, he suffered agonies of doubt and self distrust, fearing lest he be self-deceived, and again, lest he be indeed called to become a prophet of God and fail in his mission.

Here in a cave, the revelation came. Mahommed had spent nights and days in fasting and prayer beseeching God for some sign, some word that would settle his doubts and agonies of distrust and longing for an answer to life's riddle.

It is related that suddenly during the watches of the night, Mahommed awoke to find his solitary cave filled with a great and wondrous light out of which issued a voice saying: "Cry, cry aloud." "What shall I cry?" he answers, and the voice answered:

"Cry in the name of thy Lord who hath created; He hath created man from a clot of blood. Cry—and thy Lord is the most bountiful, who hath taught by the pen; He hath taught man that which he knew not."

It is reported that almost immediately, Mahommed felt his intelligence illuminated with the light of spiritual understanding, and all that had previously vexed his spirit with doubt and non-comprehension, was clear as crystal to his understanding. Nevertheless, this feeling of assurance did not remain with him at that time, definitely, for we are told that "Mahommed arose trembling and went to Khadeejeh and told her what he had seen and heard; and she did her woman's part and believed in him and soothed his terror and bade him hope for the future. Yet he could not believe in himself. Was he not perhaps, mad? or possessed by a devil? Were these voices of a truth from God? And so he went again on the solitary wanderings, hearing strange sounds, and thinking them at one time the testimony of heaven and at another the temptings of Satan, or the ravings of madness. Doubting, wondering, hoping, he had fain put an end to a life which had become intolerable in its changings from the hope of heaven to the hell of despair, when he again heard the voice: "Thou art the messenger of God and I am Gabriel." "Conviction at length seized hold upon him; he was indeed to bring a message of good tidings to the Arabs, the message of God through His angel Gabriel. He went back to his faithful wife exhausted in mind and body, but with his doubts laid at rest."

With the history of the spread of Mahommed's message we are not concerned in this volume. The fact that his own nearest of kin, those of his own household, believed in his divine mission, and held to him with unwavering faith during the many years of persecution that followed, is proof that Mahommed was indeed a man who had attained Illumination. If the condition of woman did not rise to the heights which we have a right to expect of the cosmic conscious man of the future, we must remember that eastern traditions have ever given woman an inferior place, and for the matter of that, St. Paul himself seems to have shared the then general belief in the inferiority of the female.

It is undeniable that Mahommed's domestic

relations were of the most agreeable character; his kindness and consideration were without parallel; his harem was made up for the most part of women who were refused and scorned by other men; widows of his friends. And the fact that the prophet was a man of the most abstemious habits argues the claim that compassion and kindness was the motive in most instances where he took to himself another and yet another wife.

However, the points which we are here dealing with, are those which directly relate to Mahommed's unquestioned illumination and the spirit of his utterances as contained in the Ku-ran, corroborate the experience of Buddha, of Jesus, and of all whose illumination has resulted in the establishment of a religious system.

Mahommed taught, first of all, the fact of the one God. "There is no God but Allah," was his cry, and, following the example, or at least paralleling the example of Jesus, he "destroyed their idols" and substituted the worship of one God, in place of the tribal deities, which were a constant source of disputation among the clans.

Compare the following, which is one of the five daily prayers of the faithful Muslim, with the Lord's prayer as used in Christian theology.

"In the name of God, the compassionate—the merciful.

Praise be to God, the Lord of the worlds,
The compassionate, the merciful.
The king of the day of judgment.
Thee do we worship and of Thee do we beg
    assistance.
Guide us in the right way,
The way of those to whom Thou hast been gra-
    cious,
Not of those with whom Thou art wroth, nor of
    the erring."

Mahommed never tired of telling his disciples and followers that God was "The Very-Forgiving." Among the many and sometimes strangely varied attributes of God (The Absolute), we find this characteristic most strongly and persistently dwelt upon—the ever ready forgiveness and mercifulness of God.

Every *soorah* of the *Kur-an* begins with the words: "In the name of God, the compassionate, the merciful," but, even as Jesus laid persistent emphasis upon the *love* of God, and yet up to very recent times, Christianity taught the *fear and wrath* of God, losing sight of the one great and important fact that *God is love,* and that *love is God,* so the Muslims overlooked the *real* message, and the greatness and the power and the fearfulness of God, is the incentive of the followers of the Illumined Mahommed.

The following extracts from the Kur-an are almost identical with many passages in the Holy Scriptures of the Christian, and are comparable with the sayings of the Lord Buddha.

"God. There is no God but He, the ever-living, the ever-subsisting. Slumber seizeth Him not nor sleep. To Him belongeth whatsoever is in the heavens and whatsoever is in the earth. Who is he that shall intercede with Him, save by His permission?"

The Muslim is a fatalist, but this may be due less to the teachings of the prophet than to the peculiar quality of the Arab nature, which makes him stake everything, even his own liberty upon the cast of a die.

The leading doctrine of the all-powerfulness of God seems to warrant the belief in fatalism—a belief which offers a stumbling block to all theologians, all philosophers, all thinkers. If God is omnipotent, omnipresent, omniscient, how and where and in what manner can be explained the necessity of individual effort?

This problem is not at all clear to the western mind, and it is equally obscure to that of the East.

It is said of Mahommed that when asked concerning the doctrine of "fatalism" he would show more anger than at any other question that could be put to him. He found it impossible to explain that while all knowledge was God's, yet the individual was responsible for his own salvation, by virtue of his good deeds and words. Nevertheless, it is not unlikely that Mahommed possessed the key to this seeming riddle; but how could it be possible to speak in a language which was totally incomprehensible to them of this knowledge—the language of cosmic consciousness?

Like Jesus, who said: "Many things I have to tell you, but you can not bear (understand) them now," so, we may well believe that Mahommed was hard-pressed to find language comprehensible to his followers, in which to explain the all-knowingness and all-powerfulness of God, and at the same time, not have them fall into the error of the *fatal* doctrine of fatalism.

But throughout all his teachings Mahommed's chief concern seemed to be to draw his people away from their worship of idols, and to this end he laid constant and repeated emphasis upon the one-ness of God; the all-ness, the completeness of the one God; always adding "*the Compassionate, the Loving.*"

This constant allusion to the all-ness of God is in line with all who have attained to cosmic consciousness. Nothing more impresses the illumined mind, than the fact that the universe is One —uni — (one) — verse — (song)—one glorious harmony when taken in its entirety, but when broken up and segregated, and set at variance, we find discord, even as the score of a grand operatic composition when played in unison makes perfect harmony but when incomplete, is nerve-racking.

Like all inspired teachers, Mahommed taught the end of the world of sense, and the coming of the day of judgment, and the final reign of peace and love. This may, of course, be interpreted literally, and applied to a life other than that which is to be lived on this planet, but it may also with equal logic be assumed that Mahommed foresaw the dawn of cosmic consciousness as a race-endowment, belonging to the inheritors of this sphere called earth. In either event the ultimate is the same, whether the one who suffers and attains, comes into his own in some plane or place in the heavens, or whether he becomes at-one with God, The Absolute Love and Power of the spheres, and "inherits the earth," in the days of the on-coming higher degree of consciousness, which we are here considering.

That Mahommed realized the nothingness of form and ritual, except it be accompanied by sincerity and understanding, is evident in the following:

"Your turning your faces *in prayer*, towards the East and the West, is not piety; but the pious is he who believeth in God, and the last day,

and in the angels and in the Scripture; and the
prophets, and who giveth money notwithstand-
ing his love of it to relations and orphans, and
to the needy and the son of the road, and to
the askers for the *freeing of slaves;* and who
performeth prayer and giveth the alms, and
those who perform their covenant when they
covenant; and the patient in adversity and afflic-
tion and the time of violence. These are they
who have been true; and these are they who
fear God."

Parallel with the doctrine taught by Buddha,
and Jesus, is the advice to overcome evil with
good. In our modern metaphysical language,
we must dissolve the vibrations of hate, by the
power of love, instead of opposing hate with hate,
war with war, revenge with revenge.

Mahommed expressed this doctrine of non-
resistance thus:

"Turn away evil by that which is better; and
lo, he, between whom and thyself was enmity,
shall become as though he were a warm friend."

"But none is endowed with this, except those
who have been patient and none is endowed with
it, except he who is greatly favored."

Mahommed meant by these words "he who is
greatly favored," to explain that in order to see
the wisdom and the glory of such conduct, one
must have attained to spiritual consciousness.

This was especially a new doctrine to the people to whom he was preaching, because it was considered cowardice to fail to resent a blow. Pride of family and birth was the strongest trait in the Arab nature.

In furtherance of this doing good to others, we find these words: "If ye are greeted with a greeting, then greet ye with a better greeting, or at least return it; verily, God taketh count of these things. If there be any under a difficulty wait until it be easy; but if ye remit it as alms, it will be better for you."

Mahommed here referred to debtors and creditors; as he was talking to traders, merchants, men who were constantly buying and selling, this admonition was in line with his teaching, which was to "do unto others that which you would that they do unto you."

In further compliance with his doctrine of doing good for good's sake Mahommed said: "If ye manifest alms, good will it be; but if ye conceal them and give them to the poor, it will be better for you; and it will expiate some of your sins."

Alms-giving, as an ostentatious display among church members, was here given its rightful place. It is well and good to give openly to organizations, but it is better to give to individuals who need it, secretly and quietly to give, with-

out hope, or expectation, or desire for thanks, or
for reward, to give for the love of giving, for the
sole wish to make others happy.   This desire to
bestow upon others the happiness which has come
to them, is a characteristic of the cosmic conscious man or woman.

It is comforting to know that Mahommed,
like Buddha and The Man of Sorrows; and like
Sri Ramakrishna, the saint of India, at length
attained unto that peaceful calm that comes to
one who has found the way of Illumination. It
is doubtless impossible for the merely sense-conscious person to form any adequate idea of the
inward urge; the agony of doubts and question-
ings; the imperative necessity such a one feels,
to *KNOW*.

The sense-conscious person reads of the lives
of these men and wonders why they could not
be happy with the things of the world. The
temptation that we are told came to Jesus in
the garden, is typical of the state of transition
from sense-consciousness to cosmic consciousness. The sense-conscious person regards the
things of the senses as important. He is
actuated by ambition or self-seeking or by love
of physical comfort or by physical activity, to
obtain the possessions of sense. To such as these,
the agonies of mind; the physical hardships; the
ever-ready forgiveness and the desire for peace

and love of the Illuminate seem almost weaknesses. Therefore, they can not fully comprehend the satisfaction which comes to the one who has come into a realization of illumination, through the years of mental tribulation such as that endured by Mahommed and Jesus and Buddha.

We are told that the prophet repeatedly refuted the suggestion of his adoring followers that he was God himself come to earth.

"It is wonderful," says one of his commentators, "with his temptations, how great a humility was ever is, how little he assumed of all the godlike attributes men forced upon him. His whole life is one long argument for his loyalty to truth. He had but one answer for his worshippers, "I am no more than a man; I am only human." * * * He was sublimely confident of this single attribute that he was the messenger of the Lord of the daybreak, and that the words he spake came verily from him. He was fully persuaded that God had sent him to do a great work among his people in Arabia. Nervous to the verge of madness, subject to hysteria, given to wild dreaming in solitary places, his was a temperament that easily lends itself to religious enthusiasm."

While it may be argued that Mahommed did not possess cosmic consciousness in the degree of fullness which we find in the life of St. Paul, for example, we must take into consideration the temperament of the Arab, and the conditions under which he labored. But that he had attained a high degree of Illumination is beyond dispute. This fact is evidenced by the following salient points characteristic of cosmic consciousness: A fine sensitive, highly-strung organization; a deep and serious thoughtfulness, especially regarding the realities of life; an indifference to the call of personal ambition; love of solitude and the mental urge that demands to know the answer to life's riddle.

Following the time of illumination on Mount Hara we find Mahommed possessing a conviction of the truth of immortality and the goodness of God; we find him also with a wonderful power to draw people to him in loving service; and the irresistible desire to bring to his people the message of immortal life, and the necessity to look more to spiritual things than to the things of the flesh. Added to this, we find Mahommed changed from a shrinking, sensitive youth, given to much reflection and silent meditation, into a man with perfect confidence in his own mission and in his ultimate victory.

This is the end of this publication.

Any remaining blank pages are for our book binding
requirements and are blank on purpose.

To search thousands of interesting publications like this one,
please remember to visit our website at:

http://www.kessinger.net

9 781425 324759